The Culper Ring

THE HISTORY OF THE AMERICAN REVOLUTIONARY WAR'S SPY NETWORK

Table of Contents

Introduction v

Chapter I: Background and Context...................... 1

Chapter II: Benjamin Tallmadge and
the Early Days.................................... 12

Formation of the Culper Ring 14

Chapter III: Tallmadge's Key People.................... 22

Caleb Brewster..22

Abraham Woodhull 25

Robert Townsend 27

Others 30

Chapter IV: The Ring 33

Methods 34

Early Operations 39

Chapter V: Successes and Later Years **44**
    Later Years 44
    Accomplishments 50

Chapter VI: Interesting Facts **54**
    Washington's Intelligence Background 55
    Before the Culper Ring 56
    The Role of Women 57
    Agent 355 58
    The Capture of Nathan Hale 59
    The Capabilities of the British 61
    The Restrictiveness of Secrecy 62
    Turn: Washington's Spies 63

Chapter VII: Effect and Aftermath **65**
    Impact on the War Effort 66
    Ring Members after the Revolutionary
    War 70

Conclusion **76**

Resources **79**

Introduction

Knowing is half the battle, and, in war, information can well mean the difference between victory and defeat – life and death. While this fact is perhaps more pronounced in modern warfare because of the sophistication of the intelligence apparatuses at play, it has certainly always held true. Since time immemorial, wise and successful commanders on the battlefields all over the world have always striven to know more than the enemy and to secure that crucial advantage that can only come from quality intelligence. Information, wits, planning, secrecy, and the adeptness at using the available information have all been known to decide outcomes of battles, often more so than raw power in numbers of even weaponry.

This was the case through the numerous ups and downs of the American Revolutionary War, as well. Being a competent commander, George Washington saw the value and outright necessity of intelligence gathering during the struggle against the British. Since the early days of open hostilities in 1775, the Americans made use of various channels of information and espionage to gain an edge over the often-superior British forces. A couple of years into the war, however, George Washington intensified these efforts and set in motion the formation of what would become the famed Culper Ring.

This spy ring proved to be instrumental in many key moments during the war, and it arguably altered the course of the war and thus, of history. The information gathered by the Culper Ring helped the Americans foil Britain's planned surprise attacks, ruses, economic schemes, and many other efforts that could have dealt devastating blows to the Revolution had they remained secret. As such, the Culper Ring also demonstrated ingenuity, shrewd tactical sense, competence, reliability, and commitment to victory.

The story of the Culper Ring wasn't always as well-known as it is now, which was due to much of the information about it being classified for a long time.

It wasn't until the 20th century that the public gained insight into the existence and activities of this spy network. Since then, the Culper Ring has been the object of scholarly study and discussion, especially in the US. In time, we've learned about the ring's founders, the context of its emergence, its key operatives, methods, and successes.

This is a story that weaves its way through a relatively short but decisive period in American history. Behind the main events and the history that everyone is familiar with, the story of the Culper Ring is like a seldom-told chapter that serves as an important piece of the puzzle, regardless of how it might often be overlooked. That is, however, the story that this book will recount in a concise manner so that you can remind yourself of the revolutionary heroes that went unsung for a long time.

You will take a journey more than two centuries into the past and get acquainted or reacquainted with the context, key figures, and activities of the Culper Ring, among other things. These were the inner workings of the process that gave birth to the American nation and the United States. As such, the Culper Ring didn't just influence the course of American history – it also indirectly shaped the world. Being the influential geopolitical player that it is today, the USA is a country whose history is undoubtedly world history as well.

Of course, such is history itself. It is a thread that connects the billions of dots that are the historical events that brought us to where we are. Being inseparable from each other, the events of history all lead back to those before them, no matter how indirectly. The thread that connects events can always be found if we look close enough, and seeing as this thread has led us all to the place where we are now, it also leads to the future.

CHAPTER I:

Background and Context

The tale of the Culper Ring is set against the backdrop of the American Revolutionary War and, perhaps more precisely, the British occupation of New York City. The ring didn't crop up suddenly and out of nowhere, and there is certainly a kind of continuity between the Culper Ring and earlier intelligence-gathering efforts by the rebelling colonies. These efforts were often met with failure, though, which is one of the reasons why Washington took steps to create more sophisticated intelligence networks.

Since the earliest stages of the revolution, the British occupation of New York was a major problem for the rebels. This stronghold was a constant threat, and it provided a strategically important staging area for many of the operations that the British mounted against Washington's Continental Army. All the while, Washington saw the value in getting spies into the city to bring back important information about the plans and movements of the British. Of course, this was much easier said than done.

The string of events that led to the formation of the Culper Ring can thus be connected back to the Battle of Long Island. As you may or may not know, this was the first major engagement between the British and the Continental Army after the Declaration of Independence. It also happened to be a crushing defeat for the Americans, as the British were free to move into New York City and Long Island thereafter.

Also known as the Battle of Brooklyn, this engagement took place between August 27 and 29 of 1776. This battle was sure to happen from the moment when the British had realized that they have to rip New York away from the troublesome colonies. This became especially apparent after the setbacks that the British had suffered some months before, in the spring of 1776, particularly being forced out of Boston after the Continental Army's successful siege.

The crown entrusted Lord William Howe with the task of capturing New York, and his forces also enjoyed crucial support in the form of naval superiority that the British had secured in the area. The importance of capturing New York was in the fact that such a stronghold would allow the British to drive a wedge between New England and the rest of the colonies.

Furthermore, New England was something of a hotbed for anti-British sentiment, so New York's capture was also had a psychological angle. Not to mention, New York's harbor was also an important strategic position due to its depth, which provided for a powerful naval stronghold to the side that would control the area. The British also had plans to use New York as a staging area for future northward attacks. If successful, northward breakthroughs would allow the Brits from New York to link up with their allies in Canada, creating a powerful line to separate New England from the other colonies.

Fully aware of what was at stake, George Washington did try to defend New York against the British, assigning a significant concentration of troops on his left flank, which was on the Long Island side of the East River. He also ordered his troops to construct extensive fortifications to strengthen their defensive positions. On Long Island's Brooklyn Heights, the

Continental Army's Major General Nathanial Greene positioned his divisions into a line of fortifications.

The British staged their attack from Staten Island, from where Howe planned to mount a land attack while simultaneously keeping the river blocked off. By August 22, Lord William Howe had at his disposal between 20,000 and 30,000 men comprised of regular British forces but also German (Hessian) mercenaries. On that day, all of these troops landed at the southern edge of Long Island and were poised to strike. On the other hand, the Americans amassed no more than 10,000 men at their peak during this battle. To make matters worse, General Greene's health deteriorated during this early stage, with Major General Israel Putnam taking his place. Historians generally view Putnam as a lesser commander.

The American defense was spread out thin with some two-thirds of their forces staying slightly behind to man the fortifications. The rest of the troops were tasked with taking forward positions, defending the three main roads leading to Brooklyn Heights. Howe commenced his attack during the night of August 26 and early hours of August 27 in a three-pronged strategy directing three columns of troops down each of the approaching roads.

The forward American elements were soon over-whelmed, and the survivors retreated back to the main, fortified line of defense. As the British moved in closer, they too began to dig in and build their own fortifications as a precaution. Howe didn't send his forces to attack right away, and, after the initial push, he and his army waited for two days. Before the British would mount their final attack, however, stormy and rainy weather conditions provided a window of opportunity for George Washington and his almost entirely encircled forces to escape. On the night of August 29, Washington managed to cross the East River with his troops and abandon Long Island, heading through Manhattan.

This was a very dangerous moment for the American revolutionaries. The British were well on their way toward encircling and perhaps completely destroying Washington's forces. Through tactical know-how and a bit of luck, though, Washington preserved his army, and they all lived to fight another day. It was an important moment for the revolution, especially for the morale of the rebelling colonies. Still, the battle was a definite victory for the British, who eventually controlled New York City and Long Island after Washington also withdrew from Manhattan in early September.

The human cost of the battle wasn't the worse that war has to offer, most likely thanks to the fact that Washington managed to pull his forces out and disengage. The Americans suffered around 300 dead, 800 wounded, and some 1,000 soldiers captured. The British losses were even lower, with only a bit over 60 killed in action. Had Howe mounted his final assault against the fortified American positions, the casualties would have certainly been much more devastating on both sides.

On the intelligence front, there were already some developments prior to the Battle of Long Island. The British occupied Staten Island already in June of 1776, and they did so without facing any opposition. Of course, the Patriots were well aware of the British presence and their impending attack later that summer, so there was a lot of interest to try and acquire some valuable information about the British activity on Staten Island. Indeed, Washington had certain informants working there, one of whom was Lawrence Mascoll. Spies like Mascoll provided information that was somewhat useful, but it was ultimately ineffectual as far as the outcome of the subsequent battle was concerned. Still, these early efforts did set the stage for more sophisticated measures that would come later.

Not long after the evacuation from Long Island, General Washington took steps to establish a more effective spy network or, more precisely, a channel of information from Long Island. Washington entrusted the task to Brigadier General William Heath and General George Clinton of the New York militia. This wasn't yet an attempt to establish a permanent spy operation behind British lines, but it was definitely the first big step toward more concrete intelligence work.

One of the most important developments in regard to the subsequent formation of the Culper Ring was the fate of Nathan Hale. Hale was a young man in his early twenties and was serving the Continental Army as a lieutenant. Before the Revolution, Nathan Hale was merely a teacher, but that meant he was educated, which afforded him a position among the officers when he joined the cause. In September of 1776, Hale bravely volunteered for a daring, dangerous task of crossing into Long Island and gathering valuable intelligence on the movements and plans of the British forces there.

Things went south soon thereafter, and Hale's clandestine mission was compromised. After his capture, the British took Nathan to Howe's headquarters in New York, where he was questioned, charged with espionage, and promptly executed via hanging on September 22. The news of this event reached Washington when the British themselves sent a messenger to let the Americans know.

The British officer, Captain John Montresor, provided the Patriots with details as to what exactly happened, and this story was later recalled by Captain William Hull. Namely, Hale had managed to gather quite a lot of useful information before he was apprehended. He acquired sketches of important British fortifications and their positions, for instance. Unfortunately for the Continental Army, he would never get to relay this intelligence to Washington, and it was instead taken by the British after he was arrested. When he was brought before William Howe, Nathan didn't try to hide his intentions or his purpose from his captors. He quickly stated his rank (Captain at that point), allegiance, and true motive for crossing the British lines.

Howe's response was swift just the same, and he ordered Hale to be executed the very next day without any trial or similar proceedings. The British Provost Marshal, who was tasked with keeping an eye on the prisoner, was reportedly a cold individual with little sympathy for Hale, even refusing to allow the young man to be visited by a priest or receive a Bible. The British officer and messenger who told this story to the Americans did not hide his disapproval of the way Hale was treated, and he also noted his admiration for how Hale carried himself through these rough moments.

On the day of the execution, Captain Montresor told the Americans, Nathan Hale was allowed to write two letters, one to his mother and the other to his brother officer. Hale's execution by hanging was routine and was carried out without any sort of spectacle, but his last words have been etched in history and the American national memory forever. In this famous yet simple address, Hale said, "I only regret that I have but one life to lose for my country."

After young Nathan's death, Washington was all but blind as he had no means to gather valuable information about the enemy. Despite the setbacks, he still wanted to develop this aspect of the war effort, but he changed his approach and mentality on the subject. Namely, Washington realized that, instead of risking military personnel who were more vulnerable to being discovered and caught, he should turn to civilians for intelligence gathering. It was a subtler approach as the civilians were already living on locale and would thus never stand out as outsiders. They simply attracted much less attention, and, with a bit of guidance from Washington's officers, civilians could make ace spies.

This plan slowly evolved, and the methods were improved upon through 1777. Early during that year, Washington sought council with Continental Congressman William Duer to decide who the new agents would be. On Duer's advice, Washington employed Nathaniel Sackett, a New York local, as the new spymaster who would be in charge of building a network of civilian spies and informants. Sackett was to direct these people in the field and report back to Washington and Duer. There also was a sort of intermediary between them, who functioned as the main military contact for the spies.

During the spring of 1777, Sackett's ring did manage to acquire some useful information for General Washington, but the spymaster's overall performance wasn't satisfactory to Washington. Sackett was relieved of his post soon thereafter, and Washington turned to Benjamin Tallmadge, hoping that he could perfect Sackett's work and build a truly effective spy network. This was perhaps the moment when the seed was planted, and the emergence of the Culper Ring became a matter of time, with Benjamin Tallmadge playing the main role.

Tallmadge initially picked up where Sackett left off, and he coordinated with other agents, but the year 1777 was still a year of numerous failures for the Patriot cause. Even though Sackett's earlier efforts had managed to shed some light on the planned British campaign against Philadelphia, the Continental Army was still defeated at the Battle of Brandywine on September 11, and the British seized Philadelphia two weeks later. For a while thereafter, Washington's growing intelligence apparatus shifted focus to Philadelphia, but this didn't last long since Howe decided to move his headquarters back to New York during the following year.

While all of this was happening in the early years of the Revolutionary War, the Culper Ring's soon-to-be founder was already fully immersed in the struggle. Benjamin Tallmadge's story is a prominent story of the American strife for independence, and the eventual formation of the Culper Ring in 1778 is inseparable from the man, which is why we will take a look at this biography in the next chapter.

CHAPTER II:

Benjamin Tallmadge and the Early Days

Benjamin Tallmadge was born right where he was needed on Long Island, on February 25, 1754. He was born to Benjamin Tallmadge Sr. and his wife Susannah into what would later become a sizeable family, as young Benjamin was the second of five sons. Benjamin's father, Reverend Benjamin Tallmadge Sr., was a clergyman in New York, and his family was an upstanding one. Thanks to this, Benjamin would later acquire a good education at Yale University, on top of the education that he received from his father during his formative years.

Rev. Tallmadge was a well-connected man who would often get visits from some rather important individuals. Such was also the instance when the then- President of Yale University visited with the Tallmadge family when young Benjamin was only a child. He deemed the boy as qualified to enroll in college at a young age of twelve or thirteen, but his father postponed that until he was around fifteen. Tallmadge's time at Yale was crucial for his education, but it also helped him establish important connections. One such connection was with Nathan Hale. Benjamin Tallmadge was at Yale until 1773, after which he became a teacher in Wethersfield, Connecticut.

As the American Revolutionary War drew nearer during those tense times, Benjamin Tallmadge felt more and more sympathetic toward the cause of the rebelling colonies. After the Battles of Lexington and Concord, which were officially the first engagements of the war, Tallmadge began to consider if he should join the army and do his part. The opportunity to do just that was presented to Tallmadge in 1776. Because of his stature and education, Tallmadge was offered the rank of lieutenant in the Continental Army in Connecticut by Captain Chester of Wethersfield.

Tallmadge's first taste of combat came during the aforementioned Battle of Long Island in August of that year. Tallmadge's loss during this engagement with the British was more than just the battle itself. Namely, William, Benjamin's older brother, and first son in the family were captured by the British and would meet a tragic end later on when he died in captivity. In his memoirs, Benjamin Tallmadge explained that his brother starved to death.

These setbacks aside, Benjamin proved himself very capable on the battlefield and was quick to rise through the ranks. By early winter of 1776, he was already promoted to captain and assigned to the 2nd Continental Light Dragoons, under Colonel Elisha Sheldon. At that time, this regiment was new, being established on December 12, but belonging to it was an important feat. The unit began to see more action in the spring of 1777, and Tallmadge soon reached the rank of major by April. The year of 1777 saw to it that Tallmadge was thrown into numerous other bloody encounters with the British, notably at the Battle of Brandywine and the Battle of Germantown in autumn.

Formation of the Culper Ring

When George Washington appointed Tallmadge to replace Sackett, his job description was fairly straightforward: Fulfill the role as director of military intelligence and secure information about British activity in

New York City. At the time when the focus of Washington's intelligence efforts shifted from Philly back to New York, the Patriots' spying capabilities in the city were very weak, so Tallmadge was about to have his hands full. Another reason why Tallmadge was employed by Washington's intelligence circles from the early stage was that he was a friend and classmate of the late Nathan Hale.

Things began to take off during August of 1778 when Washington received correspondence from one Caleb Brewster. Brewster, a friend of Tallmadge, was a Lieutenant at Norwalk, Connecticut, and he was offering to work as a spy. Through August, Brewster provided valuable information about the status of British naval forces, and he also informed Washington about important troop movements. Tallmadge would later function as a sort of handler for Brewster, but at this time, that role was entrusted to General Charles Scott. He was also told to recruit new spies.

History has recorded Scott as a man who didn't particularly care for intelligence work, and Washington was aware of this, which was why he also assigned Tallmadge to assist him. It wasn't just that Scott was uninterested; he was also busy with many other duties, which usually left Tallmadge in charge. Scott was old school when it came to matters of spying, and he and Tallmadge often didn't see eye-to-eye. Scott's approach to spying was simply the old-fashioned way of sending individual soldiers to scout out enemy positions.

Scott's strategy would sometimes lead to the capture and execution of these soldiers, and, just as importantly, the strategy didn't really provide a consistent and accurate stream of information. In September of 1778, Scott sent five scouts into New York only to lose three of them. Over time, it became increasingly clear to Washington that Tallmadge was the better man for the job, and Scott resigned in late October of the same year, giving way to Tallmadge as the new director of intelligence.

By November of 1778, George Washington instructed Benjamin Tallmadge to intensify his efforts toward building a sophisticated intelligence network in New York. This was essentially the official order to construct what would later become the Culper Ring. Tallmadge later reflected on these developments in his memoirs, but, confidential as he was, Benjamin didn't reveal much in his writing. All he had to say about the job was that he was instructed to establish private communication with certain people in New York, and he also noted that these channels remained open for the duration of the war.

History has made these people known to us, and most of them were Tallmadge's friends. Apart from Caleb Brewster, there were also Abraham Woodhull, Anna Strong, Austin Roe, and others. These initial recruits formed the basis of the Culper Ring, which would later grow much more elaborate than that. Abraham Woodhull was initially to serve as Brewster's contact, but he had something of a turbulent past. He was involved in illegal trade and was arrested for the crime in Connecticut before joining the ring.

The governor, however, released him on Tallmadge's request, but a man with such a record wasn't easy t0 trust. Tallmadge had to do some convincing, but Washington ultimately gave the green light to recruit Woodhull. Washington also came up with the "Samuel Culper" pseudonym for Woodhull, based on Culpeper County in Virginia. The significance of this place was in the fact that George Washington worked there as a surveyor when he was a young man.

Of course, Woodhull's alias also gave a ring its name. Tallmadge's alias, on the other hand, was John Bolton. Each time a new member was recruited into the ring, he or she would bring in other contacts. For instance, it was Woodhull who would later recruit another prominent member, Robert Townsend. These people had to be thoroughly vetted, of course, but this was how the ring grew over time.

The meticulous way in which the ring was constructed and gradually expanded was a big change of strategy when compared to intelligence efforts early in the war. Those single-trip missions involving individual scouts infiltrating New York from outside had resulted in numerous captures and executions other than just Nathan Hale, and it was a problem even before Scott took over. Tallmadge's operatives, on the other hand, were stationed in British territory indefinitely, and they had very believable natural cover stories. These were often local folks who were already members of their communities in New York.

As far as records show, not a single one of Tallmadge's spies were ever compromised. It seemed that the man had a knack for intelligence work, whereas some of the other officers whom Washington had working in his intelligence service performed poorly. Tallmadge's spies were shop keepers, local working people, family people, and other seemingly innocuous, regular folks whom the British never suspected.

At any rate, it could be argued that Caleb Brewster was the first of the core Culper Ring members who'd come under Tallmadge's command. He excelled ever since he first got in touch with Tallmadge, but this probably came as no surprise to Tallmadge. Not only was Brewster a friend of his, but they also knew each other since childhood. The same was true for Abraham Woodhull, and all three men were born in Setauket, northern Long Island, just like numerous other members of the ring throughout the years of its operations.

These initial members who formed the core of the ring didn't just trust each other in combat or with secrets – they trusted each other's judgment. As it turned out, they were right to do so since their judgment was usually on point. This was crucial for the safe expansion of the Culper Ring over time. Key members could recommend informants and reach out to them, thus vouching for them in the eyes of the other ringleaders.

The ring's work was undoubtedly made easier by the fact that New England was one of the most pro-Patriot parts of the colonies, but loyalists were still certainly plentiful and not to be underestimated. And the British themselves, of course, was a force to be reckoned with, so the Culper Ring's effectiveness and successfully maintained secrecy were owed to the ring's competence and adeptness at spying, not British incompetence.

Of course, it's also important to note that, like in any war, counter-intelligence was just as important as spying. The Culper Ring and Washington's other agents also had the job of combating British attempts to spy on the Continental Army. They had to identify infiltrated agents as well as possible traitors within their ranks. Washington valued the secrecy of his own plans just as much as he valued the knowledge about the plans of his enemy.

After a while, George Washington himself didn't even know the names of many folks in the spy network. This was because Washington wanted to give autonomy to the Culper Ring but also for security purposes. Of course, Washington was also incredibly busy and preoccupied with all sorts of war-related matters every single day, so he couldn't really keep tabs on every single informant even if he wanted to. Luckily, the men he selected to be the ringleaders were very good at getting this job done for him.

All in all, time showed that there was no shortage of brave Patriots who were willing to risk everything to help the cause. The revolutionaries didn't have to threaten or coerce people into spying for them, as they often had the sympathies of the locals who were more than happy to feed them information.

The truth is that the British weren't exactly helping their own cause with the colonists. There was a pervading perception among many British officers that New England was a hotbed of separatism and bad influence for the rest of the colonies, and these feelings bred contempt. Some British officers felt that the colonists should be dealt with harshly, and they didn't shy away from using terror tactics. Every time such violent incidents occurred, of course, new revolutionaries were created, and, in a few short years, the Culper Ring had eyes and ears everywhere they needed them.

As you can see, there were numerous key players involved in the formation of the Culper Ring, and they definitely made crucial contributions to getting the network off the ground. All of these brave individuals were competent and trustworthy in their own right, but they also functioned well as small parts of a much greater effort toward liberation. In our next chapter, we will take a quick look at the individual lives and backstories of some of these important individuals and how they made their way to Washington's intelligence service.

CHAPTER III:

Tallmadge's Key People

Before we proceed with the story after the formation of the ring and delve into its clandestine activities, we should take some time to make mention of the lives of the people that made up that ring. In the previous chapter, you've learned about how these folks played a part in the formation of the Culper Ring, but now we'll explore a bit further into their own lives and how they came to be recruited into Washington's intelligence.

Caleb Brewster

Caleb Brewster was born in 1747 in Setauket, as mentioned earlier, and he was a descendant of William Brewster, one of the passengers on the original

Mayflower ship in 1620. As a young boy, Caleb Brewster had a fascination with the sea, and he harbored ambitions of traversing these vast waters in search of adventure. When he grew up, he made his dream a reality and became a seaman, sailing to Greenland, and even London before the Revolutionary War even happened. As such, Brewster was a very competent seaman by the time hostilities began.

He returned to America in 1776 and joined the 4th New York Regiment. One of the things that made Brewster particularly valuable was his familiarity with stretches of coastline on Long Island and around Fairfield and present-day Bridgeport. Brewster used this knowledge during his service in the Culper Ring, where he was navigating the coastline with whaling boats and carrying important messages between the agents of the ring. Caleb also smuggled materials, supplies, and other things across the Long Island Sound.

These trips were very logistically important, and Caleb Brewster's contribution to the Patriot cause came at great risk to himself as each of the trips was very dangerous. His intimate knowledge of the coastlines he navigated tipped the odds in his favor, though, as Brewster was able to make use of coves and channels that most other people would avoid. Brewster proved himself an expert navigator and an incredibly adept smuggler and courier who could always be counted on by his brothers and sisters in arms.

Long Island Sound was very dangerous during the war as it was a place of significant activity by both sides. Not only was Brewster able to navigate past the dangers and take evasive action when needed, but he also sometimes attacked British ships even when outmatched. There could hardly be a raid against the British anywhere near or on Long Island without Caleb Brewster taking part in it.

Like many other members of the Culper Ring, Caleb Brewster also participated in high-profile, conventional combat operations in addition to his espionage work. In January of 1777, for instance, Brewster belonged to the 2nd Continental Artillery, where he was a lieutenant at that time. Brewster participated in the Battle of Setauket, the capture of Fort St. George, and many other engagements, generally under the command of Tallmadge in combat, just like in espionage.

As necessary as direct espionage and infiltration were, all the spies in the world wouldn't have been of much use to Washington without a reliable and consistent channel for all that gathered information. That's where people like Brewster stepped in. Brewster kept the stream of information alive and flowing, and he and the other couriers were the lifelines of the whole operation.

Through his many contributions, some high-profile and some flawlessly secretive, Brewster rightfully earned the status of a Revolutionary War hero. Those who knew him also noted that he was a clever man who also possessed a sense of humor beloved by all around him.

Abraham Woodhull

Abraham Woodhull was born in 1750 to Judge Richard Woodhull and his wife, Mary Woodhull. One of his ancestors, Richard Lawrence Woodhull, was a rather successful and wealthy settler in Setauket, so his family was quite upstanding in their community. As the Revolutionary War went on its way from 1775, Woodhull didn't immediately rush to join the fray like many of his peers. His parents were old, and he was their only son, so he spent some time tending to family matters and maintaining the family homestead, even though he did spend a few months in the Suffolk County, New York militia as a lieutenant in 1775.

Despite all that, the events around Abraham seemed to want to push him into the war. Things escalated when his cousin and Brigadier General of the New York militia, Nathaniel Woodhull, who was killed in captivity in 1776. This infused Abraham with the deep anti-British sentiment, but he still felt that he was more needed at home than in the war. On top of all that, Abraham's father was an advocate of colonial independence.

The most decisive factor in Woodhull's war destiny was perhaps his friend Tallmadge, who not only was born and lived in the same town but was essentially Woodhull's neighbor. That destiny began in the summer of 1778 after his trouble with the law, as we discussed earlier. Halfway into 1778, Woodhull started traversing the Long Island Sound and going into New York to trade. Seeing as New York was held by the British, the Patriots generally saw this as trading with the enemy, even treasonous. Revolutionary justice caught up with him in July when he got caught red-handed by an American naval patrol.

His chance at redemption came in the form of early release by order of Governor Jonathan Trumbull, who was talked into pardoning Woodhull by Tallmadge. Benjamin Tallmadge visited Woodhull to bring the good news in what was probably an unexpected reunion with a neighbor that Woodhull remembered from his town. Now, however, Tallmadge was uniformed and offering Woodhull the join the Patriot cause as a spy. Abraham's trade connections with the British were a great asset to the Culper Rind, and Tallmadge, the shrewd spymaster that he was, saw great potential in that.

We don't know the details of this meeting or how much convincing it took, but Tallmadge did talk Woodhull into joining the spy network. The British garrisons on Manhattan were reliant on the farms on Long Island for a significant portion of their supplies. One of those Long Island farmers was Abraham Woodhull, and he was to continue selling and buying his goods while keeping an eye out for what the British forces were doing. The risk was immense, but Woodhull had been leaning toward the Patriot cause for a while already. The favor that Tallmadge did to Woodhull by getting him released and also prior events that had stirred up Woodhull's feelings toward the Brits probably played a part in his consideration of Tallmadge's offer.

Robert Townsend

Robert was born in November of 1753 in Oyster Bay, New York, as the third son among eight children born to Samuel Townsend and his wife, Sarah. Robert's father was a politician belonging to the Whig Party, and he also owned a store in town. The early life of Robert Townsend is a bit mysterious, but he spent most of his years on the family homestead. As a teenager, Robert's father enrolled him in an apprenticeship at a firm called Templeton and Stewart, where he could learn to become a merchant.

Robert indeed grew up to become a merchant, but he was also a journalist to boot. In the early stages of his adult life, Robert was more preoccupied with business and his career than with notions of patriotism and the like. Just like in Woodhull's case, though, Robert Townsend's outlook on the happenings in the colonies and the Patriot cause, in general, would gradually change. As we briefly mentioned earlier, Townsend was recruited by Woodhull, but it was a while until this happened, and Townsend wasn't there from the start. Furthermore, the fact that he was recruited by Woodhull ("Samuel Culper") led the ring to give him the pseudonym of "Samuel Culper Junior," with Woodhull becoming Senior thereafter.

Robert was Abraham's friend, but this wasn't the only factor that pushed him toward the revolutionaries. Robert was already getting influenced by contemporary sources such as Thomas Paine's *Common Sense,* which advocated independence and rationalized the position. Like many others in those days, Robert also had negative personal experiences with the British or, more precisely, his family did because they were harassed.

One of the problems standing in the way of Robert's full accession to the Patriot cause was his Quaker upbringing given to him by his father. The pacifist philosophy of the contemporary Quaker teachings simply prohibited Robert from engaging in violence, even against the British occupation. However, this was also a time of important shifts in the Quaker schools of thought, and Robert soon found himself more and more inclined to believe that taking part in the Revolutionary War was justified. Historians believe that it was *Common Sense* that pushed him over that edge, in addition to the injustices that his family had suffered at the hands of British forces.

Townsend was recruited by Woodhull in June of 1779 when he was 25 years old. When it came to being incognito, Townsend was better positioned than even Woodhull himself. Not only was Robert a merchant in New York, but he also ran a coffeehouse that was frequented by British military personnel. The interactions he engaged in through these businesses were invaluable sources of information. On top of all that, Townsend made his cover even stronger by occasionally working as a columnist for the Royal Gazette, which was a loyalist newspaper. He could feign support for the Crown but also use his position as a journalist to extract even more information.

Others

These were the big three, and they are usually the first ones to be mentioned when the Culper Ring is being discussed. Of course, there were plenty of other brave folks who certainly deserve to be remembered.

Earlier, we mentioned Anna Strong as well. She was born Anna Smith Strong in 1740, in Setauket just like the others. Anna Strong seems to have been an important signaler who would often relay information to the likes of Woodhull when they would come in to trade. She sent signals via her laundry line as well, using specific combinations of clothing articles to relay certain messages, often signaling to Brewster and Woodhull and helping set up meets.

Anna was married to Selah Strong, a captain in the New York militia in 1776, when he was imprisoned by the British. Through most of the Culper Ring era, Selah remained in prison while Anna Strong carried out spy duties that they were both later paid for by Washington after the war. Anna's participation or the extent thereof has not been fully cleared up to this day, however, and a lot is still left to speculation and scholarly debate.

There is also the matter of Agent 355, who was a confirmed female operative for the Culper Ring, but whose identity is still mysterious. Some believe that this was Anna Strong, though, but there are also indications that this theory is wrong. Judging by some accounts and correspondence, this mysterious female agent seems to have been a New York socialite with important contacts with British intelligence.

A wide network of many other civilians was instrumental in making the Culper Ring's activities possible and safe. The ring's members would often elicit the help of their relatives and siblings, as well. Abraham Woodhull, for instance, would often stay at his sister Mary's boarding house, which was owned by her and her husband, Amos Underhill.

Another important member was Austin Roe, yet another merchant who maintained his business during the Revolutionary War. Some of the other names include Hercules Mulligan, a tailor, and James Rivington, who was a journalist. Rivington was also involved with the coffee house where Townsend gathered intelligence, and he was the printer of the Royal Gazette.

The extensive network of active spies and passive informants only grew larger and more interconnected as time went on. People brought in their relatives, friends, and other loved ones whom they trusted. The struggle was finding new Patriots all the time, and the British-occupied lands were soon teeming with liberty-minded conspirators who shared the dream of independence.

CHAPTER IV:

The Ring

While the people on the ground were the backbone of the ring, it was the brains behind the operation that created the infrastructure of the network. The Culper Ring's approach to spying, their methods of staying covert, and all of their other tactics were results of meticulous planning and strategizing by the gifted minds of the ringleaders. This system was what made up the other half of the operation and complemented the expertise of Tallmadge's spies in the field. We will take a closer look at how this whole intelligence machine operated in this chapter, as well as some of their more distinguished early activities.

Methods

In the beginning, Tallmadge, as the director, and Brewster, as the main navigator and courier across the Long Island Sound, was in charge of getting the information back to Washington and keeping the system going. The first actual spy was Abraham Woodhull. After gathering the desired information, Woodhull would take the message to Brewster via a meeting in Long Island. After that, it was up to Brewster to cross the Sound and meet up with Tallmadge back in Connecticut, usually in Fairfield. This simple and straightforward system became more sophisticated as the network grew, but that was the basis of how they operated.

The Culper Ring gathered all sorts of information pertaining to the British military presence. They didn't just count the number of Red Coats and watch out for major upcoming offensives. The spies kept tabs on all sorts of movement and activity, departures, arrivals, positions, and overall strength. They even reported on the morale of the British and gathered information about their supply lines and incoming shipments. Sketches were also very important, and spies would sketch things like fortifications whenever they could.

Keeping the identities of the operatives hidden was, of course, the top priority when it came to staying safe. Aliases like those of Woodhull and Townsend were used extensively, and Washington often had no idea of who many of his spies really were, as the members of the ring would refer to each other by those aliases only.

Being the crafty spymaster that he was, Tallmadge even came up with a system of encryption that was used in their reports but also to protect the personal information of the ring's members. With names and a range of other things, they used a numerical substitution system, where certain words were replaced by certain numbers. There were 763 such codes in total, each representing a certain thing. 711, for instance, represented George Washington, but they also had codes for places and factions, such as 745 for England or 727 for New York. Abraham Woodhull (Samuel Culper Sr.) was 722, while Culper Jr. was 723, and so on.

710 of 763 codes translated as specific words while the rest referred to names and places. This was essentially a book of codes that were developed by Tallmadge and given out to spies to learn. With the words and relevant names or places found in that codebook,

one could put together a letter saying quite a lot of things using only numbers. The Culper Ring's ciphers got even more sophisticated after that too. Tallmadge and Washington devised a system of replacement for each letter of the alphabet with numbers and other letters. It wasn't the most incredible code in the history of cryptography, but it got the job done.

Washington was often stationed at New Windsor, NY, on the mainland, which meant that there was British-controlled territory to traverse whenever a courier had to go there from Long Island. Couriers like Austin Roe, for instance, would go to New York City and visit Townsend's coffee house. This was where Austin Roe and others would leave messages, usually orders from Tallmadge and the like. All such orders and messages were coded and signed with pseudonyms like John Bolton, Samuel Culper Junior, et cetera.

When messages had to be taken back to Setauket, couriers would simply hide them in the goods that they were transporting and smuggle the information out of the hostile territory. In Setauket, messages would usually be hidden on or close to Woodhull's farm in designated spots where he knew to look for them. Furthermore, when another courier such as Caleb Brewster had to pick up the message then and take it elsewhere, they would know to look for the document because of the signals given by the likes of Anna Strong. As we mentioned earlier, she would do so by putting up specific clothing articles on her laundry line outside. These signals were even used to instruct Brewster, which exact cove he should use to land, as he could see Anna's clothesline on approach.

The ring's operatives were expected to be capable of improvisation in the field as well since their work always carried the risk of unforeseen circumstances where one would have to think on their feet. The British ran their counter-intelligence operations since they were well aware that American spies were operating in the field. The Culper Ring proved too sophisticated and crafty for these British attempts to catch them, but there were certainly plenty of close calls.

On one occasion, Brewster demonstrated the ability to improvise and overcome quite well. While he was waiting to meet another ring member and exchange information, he was discovered by a British officer who immediately suspected foul play and moved to apprehend the man. Brewster attacked swiftly and knocked the officer off his horse, after which he also robbed him to ensure that the British saw this incident as mere banditry instead of spying.

That wasn't the only instance when Brewster came close to being captured, though. In fact, some historians believe that the British had quite a bit of information about the man but were just incapable of catching him. It's possible that the British knew Brewster's real name and even his place of residence, and some scholars believe that the Brits identified him as the main spy courier crossing the Long Island Sound on a regular basis. Nonetheless, crafty and clever Brewster consistently eluded capture, and he even fought off multiple attempts by the Brits to apprehend him.

The Culper Ring also used other means of staying secretive. One example is an invisible ink, which was special ink that required certain chemical compounds to be applied in order to read what was written. Along with other creative ways of hiding sensitive documents and writings while smuggling them, this worked very well and minimized the amount of information that fell into British hands. It wasn't uncommon for these invisible messages to be embedded into regular letters. There are indications in the correspondence between the ringleaders that the use of invisible ink was incredibly widespread in the Culper Ring.

All in all, one of the most important aspects of the Culper Ring's methodology was the fact that their spy activities were always embedded into regular, justifiable activities that had nothing to do with their plots. The members of the ring went about their daily lives, taking care of business, running errands, and engaging in other normal activities, all while working for the Patriotic cause on the side.

Early Operations

Abraham Woodhull, for instance, was already hard at work by autumn of 1778, beginning to spy for the Culper Ring in October of that year. Tallmadge had him crossing into New York every few weeks on business, which led him into the company of British soldiers quite easily. Woodhull turned out to be a talented spy, and he took the initiative in some instances as well, giving the operations a personal touch.

Woodhull also took a public oath of loyalty to King George III in Setauket. Through October, Woodhull provided Washington with information about the strength of the British military presence and their supply status, with which the Brits sometimes had problems. He continued to do this through next month, too, also giving information about the activities of local loyalists.

Woodhull got better and better at this as time went by. He sent a very comprehensive report to General

Washington in February of 1779. The Continental Army now had insight into the strength and numbers of both the British land forces and the navy. They knew about their potential reinforcements, plans, supply lines, and much else. The following month, Woodhull's information helped the colonials learn about a planned British raid against New London, Connecticut. Furthermore, while he was staying with his sister at her boarding house in New York, he recruited her husband, Amos Underhill, to gather information as well. This boarding house was frequented by British lodgers as well, so Amos quickly proved to be a very useful spy.

Tallmadge was very satisfied with Woodhull's performance, and he soon added other couriers to assist in the transportation of letters, which sped up the process significantly. As effective as Woodhull was, though, the life of espionage was a major burden on his mind. He was reportedly under a lot of stress, always anxious, and even paranoid. By the spring of 1779, Tallmadge reported to Washington that Woodhull was anxious and increasingly unwilling to participate.

Not long after that, Woodhull met with Tallmadge back in Setauket and addressed some of his concerns.

Woodhull's worried mind was soothed somewhat when Tallmadge introduced him to invisible ink. Washington acquired this ink thanks to Sir James Jay, who was the brother of a member of the Continental Congress, John Jay. It was Washington who came up with the idea of using invisible ink that could only be revealed by scrubbing the letter with special chemicals, but James Jay helped make it a reality. Procuring this ink for the Patriots' cause was risky, though, so jay could only acquire and deliver small amounts at a time, which made the ink fairly scarce and valuable in the spy ring.

The occasional lack of invisible ink would soon cause significant problems in some situations. For instance, the capture of Washington's spy, George Higday, was mostly the result of weak security measures since the arrest was conducted after the Brits acquired letters that were exchanged between Tallmadge and Washington. There was no encryption or invisible ink used on these letters, so the Brits acquired valuable information. The whole Culper Ring was at risk during that time, and it was a wake-up call to Washington, making it clear that the ring needed more invisible ink.

The pressure that Woodhull was under during that spring of 1779 was also very real. His fears were made worse when a contingent of British troops raided his family farm, although he avoided arrest because he was in New York. Tallmadge and Washington soon began to consider whom they could recruit to replace Woodhull gradually. One candidate was the aforementioned George Higday, the man who was captured after the Brits intercepted correspondence between Washington and Tallmadge. Although he later avoided execution, he was ruined as a potential operative for the Culper Ring.

In May, more than a month before these things happened, Woodhull's resolve was already shaken when he was almost caught again. He was pointed out by John Wolsey, a loyalist on Long Island, which was what led to the aforementioned raid. Acting on Wolsey's tip, Colonel John Graves Simcoe launched that operation with the intent of capturing Woodhull. Thanks to a stroke of luck, Woodhull found himself in New York at that time. However, the loyalists who raided his home were rough with his family, and Woodhull later reported that they mistreated his elderly father.

Amazingly enough, Woodhull eventually managed to wiggle his way out of this bind by getting a loyalist militia member, Colonel Benjamin Floyd, to vouch that Woodhull was an upstanding colonist, loyal to the Crown. Nonetheless, the events of that spring and summer were a strong wake-up call to already shaken Woodhull, and he soon informed his superiors that he would no longer be able to spy in New York. Still, Woodhull was a responsible and committed operative of the ring, which was why he worked on finding his own replacement and ensuring that it was a man that could be trusted. This is how Robert Townsend eventually joined the cause.

CHAPTER V:

Successes and Later Years

Even though there were probably some growing pains, in the beginning, the Culper Ring members perfected their craft as time went by. Their presence grew along with their network, and the Culper Ring became involved in more and more events that decided the course of the war. As such, the ring has had some very impressive accomplishments in the course of the war, some of which are quite famous now. In this chapter, we'll take a look at some noteworthy accomplishments of the Culper Ring and how things went later in the war.

Later Years

As we mentioned and left off above, Abraham Woodhull was looking into finding a replacement for himself in the summer of 1779 already. After the raid and the allegations brought up against Woodhull by the loyalists, Washington and Tallmadge also generally agreed that Woodhull should be taken out of New York operations. Essentially, the ring had dodged a giant bullet that summer and keeping everything exactly the same after that was just asking for trouble.

After Townsend, or Culper Junior, was established in New York City, Woodhull took on more of a leadership role, serving as Townsend's handler and main contact line to Tallmadge. As such, Woodhull mostly stayed in Setauket, but he met with Townsend in New York as well, although such occasions were rare. The system was still similar to what it was before. Townsend gathered intelligence on-location and then passed it on to couriers like Roe. The courier would get the information to Woodhull in Setauket as quickly as possible, still using subtle means such as leaving the messages in hidden, secret spots.

Woodhull would then review the intelligence, add any comments if needed, and relay it to Brewster. The ever-vigilant and available Brewster would then take the message across the Sound and make his way to Tallmadge. Tallmadge would also evaluate and comment on the information before getting it to General Washington. This system worked, but it wasn't exactly the fastest channel of information out there. Even with the addition of fast-riding couriers, it could still take a week or even more for messages to reach Washington.

Indeed, the intelligence gathering wasn't always to Washington's satisfaction, especially because of the slow delivery. In autumn of 1779, for instance, the Patriots were expecting the arrival of French naval forces, and Washington wanted information. General Washington was working on a possible naval operation to attack New York City during that time. He wanted constant updates on what the British were doing there in New York City but also throughout Long Island. Woodhull and his contacts couldn't always deliver on these requests, though. Washington often viewed Woodhull as overly skittish and cautious to a fault.

There was also some reshuffling being done among the couriers of the ring during the autumn. For a while up to that point, one of the main couriers assigned to the ring in order to speed up the transport of letters was Jonas Hawkins, who was later joined by Austin Roe. After September of 1779, though, Austin Roe would be the only main courier.

There were problems with Hawkins for a while up until that point. He was anxious and couldn't really handle the pressure of espionage work, and his paranoia often made him reluctant to act as needed. On some occasions, Hawkins had to destroy letters for fear of being captured with them, although he never was. Sometimes, Hawkins would also request especially difficult or risky meeting spots just so he could make things a bit less risky for himself.

Needless to say, that didn't sit well with the spies like Townsend, and Hawkins' competence was soon called into question. Hawkins wasn't exactly willing to take risks anymore anyway, so he and the ring gradually just parted ways, especially after Townsend explicitly refused to work with him.

In the spring of the following year, the Culper Ring would go on a sort of short hiatus. Robert Townsend, too, was becoming weary of the exalting work that espionage required, and Woodhull had been growing tired for some time, of course. The flow of intelligence from Townsend slowed down, and the recommendation to suspend operations for the time being came from Woodhull.

The Culper Ring was thus effectively shut down for a couple of months, but Washington set things

in motion again already in July of 1780. He antici-
pated the services of the ring would be useful since
the Americans were expecting another contingent of
French troops to arrive by sea later that summer.

Another interesting character that brushed up
against the Culper Ring and contributed to intelligence, especially in the later years of the war, was Hercules Mulligan. He was a member of the Sons of Lib-
erty and involved with American intelligence circles
for quite a while and before the Culper Ring was even
put together. Mulligan was first recruited into espionage by Alexander Hamilton, and his main activities
in that regard began around 1776. Mulligan usually
operated as a lone agent, but some sources suggest
that he was giving information to folks like Townsend,
which made their reports even better.

The one person that Mulligan did constantly work
with was his slave and friend Cato, described as the
"faithful accomplice" of Mulligan's. Mulligan's first
glorious moment in intelligence work came in January of 1779 when he and Cato relayed information to
Alexander Hamilton about the British plans to kidnap
or eliminate high-ranking Patriot leaders. Mulligan
came upon this information mostly by mere chance.
As the story goes, his interest was piqued when a

British officer visited his shop late one night, requesting to buy a coat immediately.

Mulligan inquired as to the strangeness of the late hour and the haste of the officer. The British officer then told him that he and others were preparing to embark upon an important mission that would capture the rebel leader by tomorrow. Apparently, the British had caught wind of a meeting that was taking place between Washington and some of his high-ranking officers, and they were going to ambush the Americans. Mulligan immediately called upon Cato and sent him to inform Washington of the plot. George Washington heeded these concerns and changed his plans, leaving the British empty-handed.

This was actually the first out of two instances where Mulligan is believed to have saved George Washington's life. The second would-be incident occurred in 1781 when Mulligan's brother received crucial information about British plans to set another trap for Washington. Mulligan's brother was involved in import and export, which often placed him close to the British military. On one occasion, the British ordered a shipment of supplies that was unusually large. When he inquired, Mulligan's brother was told that these supplies were needed for the several hundred

British soldiers that were about to ride out and set up an ambush for Washington.

Upon hearing this, Hugh Junior immediately informed his brother Mulligan, who, in turn, got that information to the Continental Army as soon as possible. Thanks to intelligence, Washington was able to avoid capture or death once again. This was just two years before the end of the war, and Washington's capture or killing could have had untold consequences for the American Revolution.

Accomplishments

The codes and ciphers we mentioned earlier were certainly an accomplishment in their own right. Traditionally, ciphers have been something that successful militaries have paid a lot of attention to, employing the greatest cryptographers possible to devise new codes and ciphers. As such, the British had a significant advantage in this area at the start of the hostilities because their cryptographers had already devised the needed codes and ciphers. The Americans, on the other hand, started out with virtually no such tool, so they had to create their own. And that's exactly what they did – quite successfully so.

One of the major accomplishments and war contributions by the Culper Ring happened during the

Washington's Intelligence Background

Because he played such a prominent role in the physical struggle to liberate the colonies from British rule and because he was such an important political figure during the inception of the United States, Washington's experience in intelligence is often overlooked. Indeed, America's glorious revolutionary general and first president had his initial encounter with the world of intelligence gathering in 1753 when he was just 21.

As would be expected during that time, Washington operated as an agent for the British colonial government, and his job was to gather intelligence about the French military presence in the Ohio Territory. This French stronghold was deemed a threat by the British as well as a potential obstacle to their own expansionist aspirations. Washington proved himself quite adept at this sort of work, and the information he brought back was often very valuable.

In his service to the British, Washington also saw first-hand the consequences of poor intelligence gathering. After witnessing a devastating British defeat at the hands of the French due to a lack of intelligence gathering, Washington noted in his journal at the time that "there is nothing more necessary than good intelligence to frustrate a designing enemy."

The things that Washington learned during the 1750s in this regard were an important part of his strategies during the Revolutionary War. He allocated significant portions of the available military funds to intelligence gathering, and he ensured that the folks on the job didn't lack anything.

Before the Culper Ring

We already mentioned that Washington's Continental Army engaged in a fair bit of intelligence gathering before 1778. One particular unit that was officially put together during that time with the purpose of engaging in espionage was Knowlton's Rangers. This elite unit was comprised of select individuals who fit a narrow profile and were suitable for this type of work.

The unit was tasked with carrying out scouting missions, reconnaissance, but also raids against the British. As such, this was a military intelligence organization, but it was also a sort of early special operations group. This is why the US Army nowadays notes the Knowlton's Rangers as the traditional parent to contemporary Army Rangers, Green Berets, and US Special Forces in general. Of course, this elite military unit, which was also a fighting force, was quite different from the Culper Ring, but it illustrates the commitment that George Washington had to espionage and intelligence gathering. All in all, George Washington was quite the master of this particular art of war, and this is why some now consider him to be the founding father of American foreign intelligence – yet another in a string of honors forever attached to his name.

The Role of Women

We've indicated this a few times through this book, but it's worth reiterating that women indeed played their part in the revolutionary spy networks. As always, women also played crucial roles in the overall war effort through their traditional roles, but that's a given.

In the Culper Ring, however, there were other brave women other than just Anna Strong. They were the wives, sisters, mothers, and daughters of the nation who risked their lives and wellbeing to help their husbands, brothers, sons, and fathers in this struggle. Women worked as inconspicuous scouts but also as couriers and messengers of all sorts.

Lydia Darrah and Catharine Moore Barry are two other examples of female informants. Lydia was instrumental in getting Washington the much-needed information about British offensive plans while they were occupying Philadelphia. Catharine Barry, on the other hand, helped the Patriots learn about an impending British attack before the Battle of Cowpens, which then turned out to be a decisive American victory.

Traditional female roles during those days afforded women spies opportunities that weren't available to most men, at least not as frequently. Women made up the majority of cooks and maids, for instance, which often kept them close to where folks eat, rest, and meet. That meant access to information as long as they were in the right place at the right time and knew how to keep an ear out. Those who were bolder could even get their hands on sensitive documents and other papers quite easily.

Agent 355

We also mentioned the mysterious Agent 355 earlier, the female spy who still hasn't been positively identified. She is one of the few prominent agents whose achievements are quite well-known while the name still remains a secret. A bulk of what we know about her comes from the correspondence between Washington and Woodhull. Also, another clue to Agent 355 being a woman is that the number 355 translates as "lady" via the encryption system used by the Culper Ring.

The code is also what experts have used discern that Agent 355 was a woman of higher social standing. It also appears that she had contact with Major John Andre and Benedict Arnold in New York. Some scholars believe that she belonged to a prominent family that was loyal to the Crown, giving her credibility among the British and access to useful information.

As far as her later life was concerned, one version of events states that she was arrested in 1780 and kept prisoner on the prison ship HMS Jersey. It appears that this was where she died, but some sources state that she also gave birth to none other than Robert Townsend's son while imprisoned on the ship. This narrative usually goes along with the theory that Agent 355 romantically involved with Townsend. No reliable records corroborate the claim of birth, however, and the facts of these events remain murky to this day.

The Capture of Nathan Hale

How exactly the British found out about Nathan Hale and how they caught up to him is a point of some contention. There are theories that involve random chance, suspicion, but also treason. Despite his high morale and eagerness to help the Patriot cause, Hale didn't have the training or the know-how to conduct sophisticated espionage missions. He was very young and sometimes naïve to boot. When he crossed into British territory on Long Island, he wore the disguise of a Dutch schoolteacher.

One version of the story states that the uncovering and capture of Hale were the work of Robert Rogers. Rogers was a British Major and an experienced officer who went through the French and Indian War and also led the Queen's Rangers. It was also said that he had a special ability to sniff out lies and plots by his enemies. As such, Major Rogers supposedly came to suspect Nathan Hale of being up to something. Rogers then manipulated Hale, gained his trust, and, according to some sources, pretended to be a spy for the Americans as well. He thus fooled Hale and made him confess unwittingly. He was captured shortly thereafter before he could make his way back to friendly territory.

Some sources also claim that Hale was betrayed and reported by his brother Samuel because he disagreed with the Patriots. In any case, when he was captured, the British troops searched him and found papers and other evidence incriminating Hale as an American spy. The rest is a tragic and sad history.

The Capabilities of the British

For a good chunk of the war, the British paid almost no mind to intelligence gathering, and they valued this aspect of warfare very little. They were essentially making the same mistakes that they used to a couple of decades earlier when Washington still served the Crown. As it happened, Washington learned from those mistakes, unlike the British.

Only in 1780 did the British improve upon their intelligence-gathering efforts somewhat. They engaged in mostly unsuccessful counter-intelligence, trying to suppress the activity of American spies. However, they also did spying of their own, inserting operatives into Congress and the Continental Army's higher echelons. Nonetheless, most historians agree that these operations were still not on the level of the Culper Ring. What's more, even when British intelligence circles did gather useful information, it wasn't uncommon for British commanders to underestimate the threats or outright ignore the information.

In 1781, for instance, the British failed to get any information about significant maneuvers by the Americans and the French, marching together to Yorktown. Things like this didn't get past Washington, and he never underestimated any of the threats that his spies revealed. Perhaps this was owed to the technically inferior position of the Patriots when compared to the British, but this due diligence proved decisive time and time again.

The Restrictiveness of Secrecy

The very fact that the Culper Ring was a major success is what makes it entirely possible that we still don't know much about them. For a spy ring to be successful, they have to be masters of secrecy, and that usually ensures that certain things are buried forever. And because the knowledge of such things is carried only by a select few individuals, the chances of these secrets being uncovered diminishes as time goes by and people depart. This is especially true for certain highly classified actions and operations.

It's likely that the only people who were aware of every single operation that the ring conducted were Washington and Tallmadge. As for the lower-ranking members of the ring, many of them were probably on a need-to-know basis, meaning that they weren't necessarily aware of the operations conducted by other ring members unless this knowledge was instrumental to their own mission. All this is to say that even if you read every book and document concerning the Culper Ring, there's still a solid chance that you didn't learn everything that happened. As you have seen, a lot of what we now know about the Culper Ring was never meant to come out, and there's bound to be a lot of information that the ring buried with more success.

Turn: Washington's Spies

The legendary exploits of the Culper Ring have piqued the interest of the public ever since the ring's story was made public, which has earned them a special place in popular culture as well. In recent years, the tale of the spy ring was revisited by an AMC television series called *Turn: Washington's Spies*. The series ran between 2014 and 2017 and was based on a 2007 book *Washington's Spies: The Story of America's First Spy Ring* by Alexander Rose.

With few historical alterations, as is normal for such mediums, *Turn* has offered audiences a refresher on these important events. Besides, after reading this book, you will be more than capable of spotting historical inaccuracies and holes in any story about Washington's spies. It had also gotten people talking about the Culper Ring for a while, bringing the nation's attention to these overlooked heroes of the Revolutionary War.

This is only one piece of media touching upon the Culper Ring, though. Throughout the decades since the existence of the ring became public knowledge, there have also been numerous books written on the subject. This spy ring is a rabbit hole that goes quite far down, and if you want to dig deeper, it's a good idea to check with certain libraries or bookstores to find these works, newer and older ones alike.

CHAPTER VII:

~

Effect and Aftermath

If George Washington or any of the members of the Culper Ring were told, back then, that we would one day have "eyes" orbiting the Earth and gathering intelligence with telescopes from space, they probably wouldn't have even been able to get a grip on the concept right away. It would probably require some explaining to get these shrewd and industrious folks of the 18th century to fathom what modern satellites are, as intelligent and competent as they were.

Progress is a somewhat strange thing that comes with time, brought to us by generations of gifted folks whose only real difference between them is the time they were born in. The intelligence community back then was no less intelligent or gifted, but the times were a whole lot different. One important aspect of the Culper Ring's legacy is thus that it was there during the early concentrated efforts to form an effective intelligence community in the United States. Nowadays, that community is one of the most sophisticated and effective intelligence networks that the world has ever known. That's not to say that that there is any sort of continuity between the Culper Ring and the CIA, for instance, but it was the first successful and meaningful intelligence community organized by Americans.

Impact on the War Effort

The extent to which Washington's intelligence networks affected the war and altered the course of history is something that's been discussed by scholars for quite a while now. Throughout this book, you have seen how the Culper Ring operated, and you had learned about the occasions when the spies had a major impact on the outcome of certain situations. As such, you can see that the intelligence work was paramount.

One thing that some historians like to point out is that General Washington wasn't very experienced in commanding large formations. At first, Washington was focused mostly on long-term strategic goals and on supplying his forces. His lack of experience in leading large armies and his army's lack of a reliable stream of intelligence about the enemy's plans and whereabouts contributed a great deal to Washington's initial failures against the British.

As the intelligence infrastructure of the Patriots got better, so did their ability to wage war successfully. The correlation was quite clear, and Washington wasn't the only one who took notice. During those days, the entire American political leadership saw the potential and importance of intelligence gathering. Congress would later take steps to bolster these efforts even further, setting the stage for the development of the sophisticated, far-reaching intelligence apparatus that the US now wields.

Still, there were other factors at play when it came to deciding the outcome of the Revolutionary War, and some historians will argue that these were far more important than intelligence gathering. For one, the Americans had a geographical advantage, which went past mere familiarity with the homeland. Even at that time, the newly declared United States of America was a sizeable country that was difficult to control all at once. The British occupying forces had to focus primarily on urban centers and important ports for sea access. Meanwhile, the rebels could often maneuver, regroup, and organize throughout the countryside undisturbed. The terrain itself was rugged as well and full of all manner of natural obstacles and problem areas like forests, hills, mountains, et cetera.

Keeping the geographical advantage in mind but also the fact that the Continental Army was often outnumbered and outgunned, Washington made the right decision to employ guerrilla warfare against the British. This was another factor that helped the colonies win their independence. The turf advantage, coupled with high morale and a strong desire for independence, thus gave an important edge to Washington.

Of course, there was also the matter of external support for the American Revolution. This support came from Britain's colonial rivals, notably France, the Netherlands, and Spain. These were powerful allies, and they contributed support both in materials and in military personnel, which is why some historians believe that this was the most important, decisive factor in the successful outcome for the revolutionaries.

With all that said, it's quite clear that the Culper Ring and other similar efforts had an impact on the war. As you have learned, Washington's valuable information also helped his allies, not just the Americans.

This information reduced casualties, helped avoid undesirable confrontations, preserved morale, and helped protect the leaders of the American Revolution. Without it, French forces could have suffered significantly greater casualties, Washington might have been killed or captured, and a whole lot of other misfortunes could have befallen the revolution.

This is why the impact of the Culper Ring is generally accepted to have been significant, if not decisive, and the brave members are rightfully celebrated. We'll never know for sure if the revolution would have been successful without it, but it's a safe guess that it would have at least been much bloodier for the Americans.

However, the strongest testament to the importance of the Culper Ring was perhaps in the decades and centuries that followed the Revolutionary War. The fact that intelligence gathering has become so important in the modern world shows us that the Patriots had their priorities just right. Think about the second half of the 20th century and the Cold War, and how much every facet of international relations and geopolitics was affected by intelligence agencies. Certainly, the Culper Ring didn't invent espionage, but they were among the successful organizations that propelled this art of war to new prominence.

Ring Members after the Revolutionary War

Benjamin Tallmadge lived a long and rather accomplished life after the war until he passed away at age 81 in 1835. When the war ended in 1783, Tallmadge retired as a Lieutenant Colonel and opened a store called B. Tallmadge and Co. in Connecticut. He also got involved in real-estate in Ohio during that time.

At the start of the 19th century, Tallmadge became a member of the Federalist Party and, under its wing, served in the United States House of Representatives. His tenure there lasted all the way until March of 1817. He still remained involved in important aspects of political life in the country, though. In 1829, for instance, Tallmadge helped defend the honor of the Connecticut Senator Uriah Tracy. Tracy had long passed away by that point, but his loyalties were called into question by John Quincy Adams and William Plumer. Tallmadge continued to distinguish himself after that, becoming the president of the Phoenix Branch Bank and later of the New York Society of the Cincinnati as well.

All the while, Benjamin Tallmadge was also raising a family. The first time he married was in 1784 with Mary Floyd, whose father was William Floyd, Governor of New York, as well as one of the signers of the Declaration of Independence. Benjamin had seven children with Mary Floyd, but she passed away long before him, and he remarried in 1808.

Due to his extensive and distinguished military service, in addition to his life and accomplishments after the war, Tallmadge was by no means low-profile. While "John Bolton's" work might have been secret, the feats of Benjamin Tallmadge were known far and wide. As such, his legacy was immense and respected, just as it is today, with halls, towns, and other things named after him.

Unlike Tallmadge, Caleb Brewster didn't marry until after the war. He married Anne Lewis, who was a girl from Fairfield, Connecticut. Brewster soon relocated to his wife's hometown and opened a blacksmith business in addition to working as a farmer. Anne Lewis was the daughter of a man who owned the wharf in Fairfield, which played an important part in many of Brewster's wartime operations.

Brewster became employed by the United States Revenue Cutter Service in 1793, which was essentially a precursor to the US Coast Guard. He spent years as an officer of this service, but he was absent from the position for some three years during the mandate of President John Adams because of political disagreements. Years later, in 1812, Brewster came to command the USRCS's revenue cutter, USRC Active. In 1816, a year after the War of 1812 came to an end, Brewster's service here ended as well.

Brewster was in command of USRC Active throughout the War of 1812, and he was doing what he did best – gathering intelligence. Navigating the seas like before, Brewster and his men gathered valuable information and brought it back to New York, particularly to Commodore Stephen Decatur. Brewster's information affected the outcomes of numerous engagements between the Americans and the Royal Navy.

When it came time to retire, Caleb Brewster settled down at his farm in Black Rock, Connecticut, where he passed away in 1827. Apart from his immense, patriotic legacy in America's early struggles, Brewster also left behind eight children by his wife, Anne Lewis.

Abraham Woodhull remained where he was before the war, on his farm in Setauket. Woodhull got married in 1781 as the Revolutionary War was slowly grinding to a halt and reaching its epilogue. His wife, Mary Smith, bore three children, but she passed away in 1806. Like many other former members of the Culper Ring, Woodhull also took up some political appointments, such as the magistrate in Suffolk County between 1799 and 1810. He also served as a Suffolk County Judge, which provided for a comfortable and fulfilled life.

In 1824, Woodhull married his second wife, Lydia Terry, even though he was already well into his 70s. He spent his last two years with Lydia before he passed away in early 1826 at age 75. He was buried in the burial grounds at his hometown's Presbyterian church.

Robert Townsend was a private man who wished to keep his espionage exploits secret and his identity hidden. To that effect, he went back into the anonymity of his family home in Oyster Bay, Long Island, and he requested from his former associates to respect his wish to remain anonymous and be left in peace. Before he went back to Oyster Bay, he severed his business ties after taking care of everything. Robert never got married, and he lived out the rest of his life in a quiet manner, along with his sister in Oyster Bay. Historians believe that Robert Townsend did have one child, although it was a son born out of wedlock, possibly to his housekeeper, Mary Banvard.

Townsend never spoke of his wartime spy activities, and his Culper Ring associates honored his anonymity, so he took his secrets with him when he passed away in 1838, or at least he thought he did. Namely, we are now aware of Townsend's identity and activities thanks to the keen eye of Morton Pennypacker, a historian who examined some of Townsend's letters in 1929. Pennypacker was examining certain letters that came from Robert Townsend's family home when he noticed that the handwriting in the letters written by Robert was very similar to that of some of the letters that George Washington had received from "Samuel Culper Jr." In the time since then, historians have confirmed that Morton Pennypacker's theory was correct.

Anna Strong, one of the few women among the distinguished members of the Culper Ring, is believed to have lived until 1812 when she passed away at 72. Not much is known about her post-war years except that she reunited with her husband. The two lived out their years in Setauket with nine children.

Most of the Culper Ring operatives and informants who survived the war lived out their lives in relative normalcy after the Revolution, each in their own unique ways. Some continued to contribute to their young American nation while others fulfilled

their lives in some more private, family-oriented un-
dertakings. In either case, the incredible espionage
work that these folks conducted during the war was
certainly enough to secure them a place in the hall of
heroic Patriots.

Conclusion

The story of the Culper Ring makes it abundantly clear that war is much more than charging the front line, blowing up a bunker, or eliminating the enemy physically. Under the turbulent, violent surface of combat, war involves wit, craftiness, communication, and a whole lot of logistics. Ever since organized warfare became a phenomenon in human civilization, spying has been an important part of it.

The realm of spies is a quiet world where sharp minds and caution govern over raw force, but it's still an incredibly dangerous world. As you have learned from this story, the members of the Culper Ring and earlier intelligence networks were brave individuals with love of homeland in their hearts and thoughts of freedom on their minds. They were prepared to sacrifice everything just to contribute to the Patriot cause and reduce American casualties. Civilians and military personnel alike, these were some of the finest individuals that America has ever produced. And while the likes of Nathan Hale have paid the ultimate price, their actions have left an irreversible mark on history and have certainly secured them their place in the halls of greatness.

What's also important to understand is that these courageous men and women didn't do any of it for the glory. In fact, they knew that, in most cases, they would receive quite the opposite. Their work had to be kept a secret, and they knew full well that the life of spies wasn't one of recognition and commendations. In most cases, that recognition came long after they had departed from this world.

The members of the Culper Ring risked their lives regardless because they believed in the cause of the Patriots, and they could envision the greatness that the future might hold for their young nation if the struggle was won. With that hope and promise, and with a lot of perseverance and struggle, these folks and the many soldiers on the frontlines carried their burden and saw to it that the war was won.

After all these years, the current generations have access to the information that shows the true extent of these clandestine efforts and how they affected the course of the Revolutionary War. We are now able to give these brave folks the recognition and glory that they deserve but couldn't receive in life. At the very least, the new generations should ensure that the memory of these true patriots lives on for as long as America does, and beyond.

Thank you for reading and hopefully you enjoyed this book!

Resources

https://www.youtube.com/watch?v=F1ChVGE00c4

https://www.youtube.com/watch?v=QgPqLBSfOVE

https://www.history.com/topics/american-revolution/american-revolution-history

https://www.britannica.com/event/Battle-of-Long-Island

http://www.eyewitnesstohistory.com/hale.htm

https://www.mountvernon.org/library/digitalhistory/digital-encyclopedia/article/benjamin-tallmadge/

https://www.thefamouspeople.com/profiles/benjamin-tallmadge-35119.php

https://www.britannica.com/biography/Benjamin-Tallmadge

https://www.ducksters.com/history/american_revolution.php

https://www.thoughtco.com/the-culper-ring-4160589

https://www.britannica.com/topic/Culper-Spy-Ring

https://www.mountvernon.org/library/digitalhistory/digital-encyclopedia/article/culper-spy-ring/

https://www.history.com/topics/american-revolution/culper-spy-ring

https://www.historyisfun.org/blog/all-about-the-revolution/espionage-and-the-culper-ring/

https://www.nytimes.com/2016/07/10/nyregion/tracing-the-origins-of-a-revolutionary-war-spy-ring-on-long-island.html

https://historycollection.co/10-significant-things-about-the-culper-ring-george-washingtons-most-important-spy-network/10/

https://www.thesslstore.com/blog/encryption-helped-win-americas-revolutionary-war/

https://connecticuthistory.org/caleb-brewster-and-the-culper-spy-ring/

https://www.mountvernon.org/library/digitalhistory/digital-encyclopedia/article/espionage-tactics/

https://www.cia.gov/library/center-for-the-study-of-intelligence/csi-publications/books-and-monographs/the-founding-fathers-of-american-intelligence/art-1.html

https://coastguard.dodlive.mil/2014/07/caleb-brewster-revolutionary-war-hero/

https://peoplepill.com/people/caleb-brewster/

https://allthingsliberty.com/2014/05/abraham-woodhull-the-spy-named-samuel-culper/

https://www.biography.com/political-figure/abraham-woodhull

https://www.nytimes.com/1985/12/15/nyregion/rememberng-a-master-spy-at-home.html

https://www.armyupress.army.mil/Journals/NCO-Journal/Archives/2018/July/Washington-Spies/

https://www.american-revolutionary-war-facts.com/American-Revolutionary-War-Spies-Facts/Culper-Spy-Ring-Facts.html

https://www.american-revolutionary-war-facts.com/American-Revolutionary-War-Spies-Facts/American-Revolutionary-War-Spies-Facts.html

https://www.american-revolutionary-war-facts.com/
American-Revolutionary-War-Spies-Facts/Na-
than-Hale-Facts.html

https://thehistoryjunkie.com/culper-spy-ring-facts/

http://www.softschools.com/facts/american_revolu-
tion/culper_spy_ring_facts/3691/

https://www.thoughtco.com/hercules-mulli-
gan-4160489